Playing
to Learn

Developing high quality experiences for babies and toddlers

Ann Langston and Lesley Abbott

Open University Press

Open University Press
McGraw-Hill Education
McGraw-Hill House
Shoppenhangers Road
Maidenhead
Berkshire
England
SL6 2QL

email: enquiries@openup.co.uk
world wide web: www.openup.co.uk

and Two Penn Plaza, New York, NY 10121-2289, USA

First published 2007

A catalogue record of this book is available from the British Library

ISBN-10: 0 335 22238 2
ISBN-13: 978 0 335 222384

Library of Congress Cataloging-in-Publication Data
CIP data applied for

Typeset by HL Studios, Oxford
Printed in the UK by Bell and Bain Ltd, Glasgow

The McGraw·Hill Companies

Contents

List of Contributors

Thanks are due to the staff, parents and children of the following settings for their involvement, contributions and support:

Bridgwater Early Years Centre, Somerset
Cruddas Park Early Years Centre, Newcastle Upon Tyne
Harvey Early Years Centre, Bolton
Tamworth Early Years Centre, Staffordshire
Thomas Coram Early Excellence Centre, Camden, London

PLEASE NOTE: Where links have been made to the Early Years Foundation Stage it should be noted that these relate to the EYFS Consultation Document, and not to the final version of the EYFS, which is due to be published in Spring 2007.

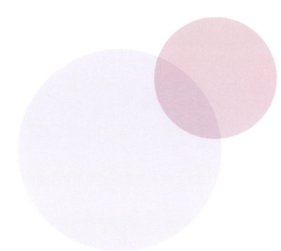

Preface

These materials were developed as the result of a project, focused on high quality experiences for children from birth to three. The project was undertaken in five early years centres in the UK and involved parents, children and practitioners in their everyday encounters with one another. The abiding message to be found in these materials is that when children play they also learn – provided that those who care for them interact with them with genuine warmth and affection and that they provide appropriate experiences that interest and engage them.

Acknowledgements

We are grateful for the support of the Esmée Fairbairn Foundation, which enabled this project to take place and to the children, parents and practitioners who kindly allowed us to use their photographs in this booklet and to film them for the accompanying DVD.

x

Introduction

Purpose

These materials are intended primarily to support practitioners, including childminders working with babies and toddlers in out-of-home settings; however, they would also be useful and informative for parents of young children.

The materials are intended to focus on significant issues relating to child care practice, particularly the provision of high quality learning experiences.

It is assumed throughout that all the examples used reflect a commitment to equal opportunities and to the development of effective partnerships between practitioners and parents.

This booklet contains a DVD.

The study topics

There are eight study topics. Each study topic relates to a chapter on the DVD and is divided into *two sections*, which can be studied separately or together.

Section A

This section comprises:

- Photographs taken from the DVD.
- A context section giving a background to the chapter of the DVD it is taken from.
- A links section detailing the related DVD chapter; relevant Aspects or Components from *Birth to Three Matters* (DfES 2002) and links to the *Early Years Foundation Stage* (EYFS Consultation) (DfES 2006).
- Discussion points.

Section B

This section comprises:

- Readings taken from relevant, informative texts, pertinent to the DVD clip, and suitable for use with groups, to stimulate discussion and act as a starting point for further reading and/or enquiry.
- Implications for Practice – a series of prompts for trainers/individuals to consider in order to determine ways of moving practice forward as a result of having studied the materials.

Using the booklet and DVD

The units can be studied by individuals or groups of people, led by a trainer, wishing to review or learn about high quality experiences for babies and toddlers.

The sequences presented in the DVD reflect everyday experiences and interactions between children and their parents or practitioners. They have been selected to provide a stimulus for observation and discussion. Additional support for the latter is also provided by the inclusion of selected readings, questions and challenges for individuals or groups to think about. It is not suggested at any point that the activities and interactions are models to be followed, rather that they illustrate how, in contingent relationships, adults who know children intimately can support their play and learning through observing them, reflecting on what they see, their provision and their own role in supporting children's play and learning. This may include modelling behaviour, words or actions, or sometimes it may be about following a child's lead; however, it will always be about observing the child in order to know what interests them so that the play experiences provided will support their learning.

The cycle which is involved in providing support for babies' and toddlers' play and learning rests on:

- Understanding how children develop.
- Getting to know the child well.
- Meeting children's needs.
- Following children's interests.
- Analysing what has been learned about the child's needs and interests.
- Providing experiences to support children's development and learning.
- Reflecting on what has been learned about the child, and on the experiences provided.
- Reviewing and evaluating the role of the adult in the child's experiences.
- Planning to meet the child's needs and interests.

Each section of the DVD has been analysed and some suggested areas for study are addressed briefly in the following pages. However, it is intended that the materials should be a flexible resource which is multi-layered, offering, to thoughtful practitioners and trainers, a number of uses. The following are ideas that individuals or trainers might wish to consider, though they are not intended to be prescriptive or inflexible – the primary purpose of this resource is to provide examples of effective practice with babies and toddlers, so that adults can reflect on the 'taken-for-granted' interactions that occur daily when children and adults are together.

Uses include using the DVD as stand-alone clips for practice of observation skills, whether by new students or by established professionals, each of whom will identify and draw different conclusions and questions about what they have seen and what issues the sequence raises for them either about children's development, play and learning or about effective practice with young children.

The DVD chapters can also be used alongside the associated Section 1 of each study topic – where a number of issues are raised relating to broad concepts addressed within the clip. In Study Topic 1, for example, 'Baby with scarves', the reader is advised to consider issues about: (a) attachment behaviour; (b) positive self-concept; and (c) policies which support babies settling in to a setting. Support about each of these issues is then provided either in the 'Effective Practice in Action' section or through the readings which follow. The same piece could, however, be used flexibly to consider relationships, resources, babies' development, interaction and so on.

A further anticipated use is that the readings can be considered either before or after watching the related DVD clips, and will form the basis of discussions. Finally, the section 'Implications for Practice' is intended to offer further challenge and questions about practice that broadly relates to the issues raised through the Discussion Points and/or the DVD clips.

Background to Effective Practice

Effective practice

'What is effective practice in providing high quality learning experiences for young children?' When asked this question many people have suggested the following are significant:

- Equal opportunities.
- Well trained adults.
- Meeting children's needs.
- Following children's interests.
- Working in partnership with parents.
- Observing children.
- Recording progress.
- Planning for individuals.
- Importance of interaction, talk, play.
- Appropriate activities, experiences.
- Appropriate environment, resources.
- Relationships, especially with a key person.

Effective practice in action

Effective practice consists of many aspects, especially those referred to in the previous responses. The following paragraphs may also be helpful in focusing on some features of effective practice with babies and toddlers.

Meeting children's needs

Children need loving, kind, sensitive adults upon whom they can depend. They place their trust in adults when their needs are met and they become attached to a small number of key people in their lives.

Attachment behaviour

Attachment behaviour, first described by Bowlby, is distinguished by the infant/child carer relationship. Bowlby noted that

the child's attachment figure appeared to provide a secure base from which the infant could safely explore and to which they could return if tired, stressed or in other form of danger or need. The attachment figure was [highly significant] in helping the infant to make sense of the social world and their availability was essential for the child's well-being.

(International Attachment Network 2002)

Self and other

A further aspect of the relationship between the attachment figure and the child is that the child then goes on to develop 'a sense of themselves in relation to others' and this understanding then guides their understanding of relationships and of social interaction.

Positive self-concept

As a result, the child then goes on to build a positive self-concept. This self-concept is based on the extent to which they feel valued, and in turn leads them to develop effective strategies for getting help when they require it, being more optimistic in terms of social relationships, and having higher levels of self-confidence and self-esteem (International Attachment Network 2002).

Knowing and communicating

The relationships that help children develop in this way rely upon the adults knowing the child well and communicating with the child. This involves observing the child, talking to the parents about the child and really watching the child as well as listening to them.

Feelings and emotions

When an adult knows a child well they are 'tuned in' to the child's feelings and emotions and they are able both to accept the child's feelings and to act as a 'container' for those feelings. In other words, adults help the child to recognize that their feelings are acceptable and will not overwhelm them, no matter how strongly they may experience them.

Well trained adults

Increasingly, research has highlighted the role of well trained adults in children's development and progress. Recently the Effective Provision of Pre-School Education (EPPE) study (Sylva et al. 2004) revealed that two of the factors impacting on high quality pre-schooling were:

- Staff having higher level of qualifications.
- Warm, interactive relationships between adults and children.

This study also highlighted the importance of the value of equal emphasis being placed in the setting, on both educational and social development.

While it is acknowledged by government that 'childcare workers already have a wealth of relevant knowledge and skills acquired through education, training, work and personal experience' (HM Treasury 2004: 45) it is important to consider how both knowledge and skills translate into practice and, in turn, impact on children's emotional well-being.

It is expected that well trained adults do what is supportive of children's all-round development, compared with, for example, newcomers, students or non-qualified staff – highlighting the significance of well planned induction training for members of the child care workforce.

Relationships, especially with a key person

Effective relationships are key to the mental health and well-being of human beings, especially babies and young children. It is through experiencing warm, caring relationships that children learn about themselves and other people. Well trained adults are aware that children play and learn in more complex ways when they are at ease in the environment, trust their caregivers and feel a sense of belonging. Effective settings place the highest importance on planning to meet children's needs by helping the child to develop relationships, especially with a key person. The key person becomes a secure base for the child, getting to know them and their families well, and acting as the main link in their experience.

Observing and responding

Observation is one of the ways we find out about anything in the world, so when babies and young children are our focus we find out about their interests, preoccupations, concerns, habits, likes, dislikes, development, relationships and many other things. We add to this sum of knowledge what we learn from the things their families share with us and tell us about them. This builds a detailed picture of the baby or young child in many dimensions as an older or younger sibling, as a grand-daughter or a nephew, as someone who loves playing with water, or feeding the ducks or who loves to play with words or is frightened of the wind, or likes to talk to relatives on the phone. We can then truly begin to respond to 'who' the child is. Our responses might include extending what we provide in the setting to accommodate this particular child's fascination with fish, or it may be about giving the child individual time to look at pictures of the people who are important in their life, but who are far away at the moment. By observing and responding to children in order to understand the way they are developing and to find out about their interest, skills and abilities and, if necessary, to identify any individual needs the child may have, practitioners gather information about children which will begin to inform their daily interactions, their communications with parents and carers and their planning.

Sensitive adults

Sensitive adults have the capacity and skill to ensure that children's emotional needs are met. Listening to and observing the child helps the adult to recognize and prevent stressful situations arising for the child. Placing the child's needs first means that the curriculum is not fixed, but organic, growing from what is appropriate for a particular child on a particular day.

Adult as a resource

These adults act as a resource for children, watching, listening, interacting with them, standing back at times, and at other times joining in with them as they play and learn.

How babies and young children learn

Knowledge of how babies and young children learn is vital to knowing what support children require in their play, and in understanding the adult's role in play. Children sometimes need nothing more than a sensitive observer who may offer a commentary on what they see, or may simply offer silent support. At other times children may want an active play-mate or one who helps them to begin to play. Play and learning are closely linked. Children's play emerges as they engage with new experiences – a fourteen-month-old who has just 'cottoned on' to what keys are for might endlessly run 'his' set of keys along the door; a child who has just had new shoes might gather every shoe in the cloakroom to play 'shoe shop'; another might be fascinated by a purse, by cardboard tubes or by pushing and pulling a baby gate. When children's play is self-chosen it has the capacity to be a 'learning experience', and, while to an adult it may appear slow and laborious it nonetheless is what helps the child to build concepts and fresh ideas about what things are, how they work and how the child, themselves, can influence outcomes. Another important aspect of how children learn is through the ongoing interaction of parents and family members, such as siblings, and carers and other adults and children. Talk helps children to express their feelings and ideas, to label, describe categorize and classify objects, and to enter into a world of possibilities and imaginative journeys. In addition children learn through observing and imitating others, through trial and error, through experimentation, through listening and through every experience encountered in their daily lives.

Imaginative play

Children need active involvement in what they are doing and this may take the form of the adult becoming a role model for the child, offering them a 'pretend' cup of tea and showing them how pretending can change from being a momentary event to something which becomes much more sustained. At other times the adult may wash the dishes for real and show the child how to make the water soapy, how to rub the dishes with a brush and rinse them when they are ready to be drained, and the child may either build on this experience, climbing up to the sink or playing with their own bowl of water and a jug, or may not be interested in pursuing that interest for the time being. Imaginative play may involve taking on roles from a story, or pretending to talk on a 'phone' made from a building block, playing at being a dog, a cat or taking on an adult role: whatever form it takes it is highly significant for children and is encouraged when adults accept children's repeated journey from reality to pretence.

Interaction, play and talk

Children learn from every interaction – they learn about themselves, relationships, about their own actions and reactions and about people and objects. They also benefit from the process of being helped to understand by a more skilful person. This understanding may result from an adult talking with a child about why something might have happened, such as why the squirrel ran away when the dog barked at it. Equally it may be about helping children to follow a sequence to put on their coat, a skill achieved over a period of weeks, possibly.

Engaging with children's emotions

Engaging with children's emotions is something that appears 'natural' yet this is a skill, like any other that may be practised and perfected over time. Children's emotions are often very obvious – easily stimulated and just as easily switched on or off when something occurs that pleases or annoys, or upsets them. Helping children to recognize their feelings by reassuring them and talking to them when they are distressed, or by sharing their joy, helps children to understand that their feelings are acceptable and can be managed.

Joint engagement

Joint engagement, a term used by Bruner, describes the involvement of the adult with the child and the child with the adult – when, through a process of co-construction, new learning is achieved as the two interact and the adult offers some form of 'instruction', though this is never formal and always occurs because the child is motivated and interested in the shared focus. This joint engagement may occur as a child and an adult look at a snail that is making its way along the path; when they may talk about it, guessing where it's going, or estimating how long it will take for it to reach the leaves growing nearby. The main characteristics of this engagement are that 'the child and mother [or adult] are actively involved with the same object or event, and the child is actively and repeatedly acknowledging the mother's [or adult's] coordination' (Adamson et al. 2004).

Following children's interests

Motivation studies reveal how levels of involvement can be sustained over long periods when an individual is intrinsically interested in the chosen subject or task in which they are involved. Ferré Laevers (1997/2004), a psychologist, describes features of engagement by three- to five-year-old children (in given tasks) indicating their levels of involvement in what they are doing. These range from Level 1, where:

- 'There is no real activity. The child is mentally absent. If we can see some action it is a purely stereotypic repetition of elementary movements'.

to Level 5, where:

- 'The child is very concentrated and really enjoys the activity. Posture and mimic express a kind of (positive) tension. The level of the performance matches the capabilities of the child. Any disturbance or interruption would be experienced as very frustrating'.

Indicators of this type can sometimes be useful in gauging children's interest in a particular activity or experience, although of course they should only be used as a guide and related to an individual child in a specific context.

Schemas

Athey (1990) describes 'schemas', or patterns of repeated behaviour, indicating a child's current interests and play agenda. Her examples include trajectory, when a child is interested in, for example, the horizontal path of projection followed by things that fly such as birds, or aeroplanes, or a ball. When a child has such an interest they may engage in activities that seem meaningless until the pattern of play is analysed when the interest will then be evident to adults.

Child's agenda

When adults follow children's interests they respect the choices children make and follow the child's agenda, not blindly but with a sense of awareness, knowing that when a child is involved and interested they are likely to benefit much more from an experience than from joining in one in which they are not particularly interested.

Appropriate activities and experiences

Appropriate activities and experiences arise from the observations and discussions of parents and practitioners and focus on children's current preoccupations and interests, such as a favourite story, wanting to pour water from one container to another, transporting sand, play-people or bricks from one place to another or mounting and dismounting from a push-along toy. Skilled practitioners understand that children need support to pursue their interests and that at times children may need them to become a play-mate, a resource provider, or an audience to their efforts.

The environment for learning and development

The environment is all the places (and the people) the baby or young child is placed in (or with) – sometimes it is inside the building, at other times it is in the outdoor play space and, occasionally, it is beyond these in places such as the street, the woods or the beach, where planned visits and outings have been planned.

The indoor environment

Babies and toddlers love to be in an interesting indoor environment where they can see and hear what is going on around them, investigate what they encounter and explore, conquer or rest in it. This environment should always be planned carefully to ensure that all children and adults can negotiate and access it safely and easily. It should be well maintained and should offer a variety of stimulating, engaging, challenging and positive experiences for all children. It should be a place where children can rest or participate and should provide materials and resources that are safe and attractive. It should be a place where the child has a sense of belonging and where they feel emotionally and physically secure and safe.

High quality resources

High quality resources are always on offer in an effective environment for learning and development. They may be expensive or inexpensive but they will offer varied use, so that babies and young children can choose how to interact with them. The most important issue in developing high quality resources is acquiring things which can be used flexibly and which are capable of withstanding a great deal of wear and tear. Maintaining resources in good order is essential.

Loving the natural environment

Babies and toddlers have a capacity to engage with the environment from the start; they build their love, respect and attitudes to the environment from their experiences of it. Adults are powerful role models who teach children about caring for and respecting the environment, both the natural and the built. Babies and young children quickly learn to enjoy being out of doors when adults show them that being out of doors is a pleasure, through all the variations of the weather and the seasons.

Study Topics

1 Baby with scarves
Section A

This is a drop-in session for parents and their children, staffed by a number of practitioners including Tony, a play worker. The baby is one of three siblings below the age of three. Their mother, who is seated close by, is interested and involved in the activities and experiences of all her children. When the sequence starts the camera has just shifted towards Tony as he joins the baby on the floor. Attending a drop-in session is often preliminary to a baby becoming a more permanent member of the nursery, crèche or child care setting and therefore is a significant event in the lives of all involved.

Links

- DVD Chapter 1.
- Birth to Three Matters: A Strong Child: A Sense of Belonging.
- Early Years Foundation Stage: Personal, Social and Emotional Development.

Discussion

After watching Chapter 1 of the DVD consider what issues the sequence raises regarding the following:

- Attachment behaviour.
- Positive self-concept.
- Policies which support babies settling in to a setting.

Section B

Readings

Reading 1.1

If a child's key person forms a positive relationship with her parent, it can form the cornerstone of a partnership between nursery and home. This relationship can build trust and deepen not only the key person's knowledge of the child, but the parent's knowledge of the child's experience in nursery – real knowledge, not just an account of nappies changed and food eaten. It can offer parents peace of mind and a feeling of inclusion, making it possible to leave their child confidently and smoothly, especially if they can develop reassuring 'coming and going' routines with their child's key person.

(Edwards 2002: 20–1)

Reading 1.2

Staying near

Seeking proximity to an adult is a key feature of an attachment relationship. Babies and toddlers show their need to feel secure through searching for their carer when they are not in sight, reaching up to be picked up, cuddling and clinging, and following or approaching their key person. These behaviours can be frequently observed in babies' and toddlers' play. The distance at which the child will feel comfortable will depend on factors such as age, temperament, developmental history, and whether the child feels tired, frightened or ill.

(Manning-Morton and Thorp 2003: 21–2)

Reading 1.3

Starting off

The settling-in period is intended to bridge the gap for the children between home and nursery. It should help them to become accustomed to the nursery and form an attachment to their key person, who will be with them for much of the time.

Preparation is the key to success so that when the time comes everybody and everything is ready to get the child off to a good start.

Getting ready

To help welcome the child it is important to create the right nursery environment which:

- Is child-friendly, homely and welcoming.
- Offers a place for children's things, such as boxes or cubby holes.
- Allows for the child's comforter to be accessible at all times.
- Presents family pictures at child level.
- Reflects diversity.

All the people involved should also be prepared.

Parents and child

- Invite them to visit the nursery before attending for the first day.
- Encourage them to talk about nursery together and recall the staff, especially the key person.
- Lend nursery toys for them to play with together.
- Get personal items ready for the first day – special bag, photograph, comforter, clothes.

Key person and parents

- Plan how the child will start in the nursery.
- Discuss routines.
- Observe special times between parent and child.
- Observe parents feeding and changing the child so staff can follow their lead.
- Share information.
- Help the child become familiar with the environment.
- Discuss how they will share the care of the child.
- Talk about how the parents' attitudes to leaving the child will affect the child's feelings.

Child and key person

- Encourage the child to spend time with the key person during the settling-in period.
- Talk about what activities the child likes to do best.
- Look at and talk about pictures of the child's family.
- Introduce the child to other children and adults.

(Langston 2003)

Implications for practice

Think about:

1 How does the setting support *adults* to cope with the settling-in process for babies as they begin to attend the setting?

- Develop policies that all staff feel comfortable with.
- Discuss at staff and team meetings how to manage parents' individual preferences for settling their babies in the setting.
- Provide opportunities for key workers to have supervision with a supervisor who can support them emotionally at times such as when a child leaves or does not relax with them.

2 How does the setting support the settling in experience for *babies* as they begin to attend the setting?

- Mentor new staff members.
- Model behaviours for students and new staff.
- Peer observation of ways of mirroring babies' behaviours.
- Prepare display showing non-verbal signals used by babies, children and adults.

Consider:

3 What practitioners might do differently as a result of watching the video and thinking about the messages conveyed through it and the readings and discussion.

- Think more about how the baby feels as they come to a new setting.
- Find new ways to support babies' play in the future.
- Show other practitioners how to follow the baby's lead.
- Review how babies and parents are encouraged to become familiar with practitioners and the setting before attending on a more permanent basis.

2 Leaves in the garden
Section A

An informal outdoor activity which takes place in the garden of a large, inner-city children's centre which offers core day and extended provision for children from six months to four years. The practitioner, Linda, follows the lead given by the children and responds to the needs and interests of a group of children of mixed ages.

Links

- DVD Chapter 2.
- Birth to Three Matters: A Competent Learner: Making Connections.
- Early Years Foundation Stage: Personal, Social and Emotional Development, Knowledge and Understanding of the World.

Discussion

After watching Chapter 2 of the DVD consider what issues the sequence raises regarding the following:

- Learning through play.
- Learning through role models.
- Loving the environment.

Section B

Readings

Reading 2.1

Schemas

Anyone who watches a young baby will see that some early patterns of behaviour (or schemas) are already evident. As babies suck and grasp, they rehearse the early schematic behaviours which foster their earliest learning. Early patterns of behaviour seen in babies become more complex and young children do not perform single isolated behaviours but co-ordinate their actions. Toddlers work hard, collecting a pile of objects in the lap of their carer, walking to and fro, backwards and forwards, bringing one object at a time. They are working on a pattern of behaviour which has a consistent thread running through it. Their patterns of action and behaviour at this point are related to the consistent back-and-forth movement. The early schemas of babies form the basis of the patterns of behaviour which children show between the ages of 2 and 5 years, and these in turn become established foundations for learning.

(Nutbrown 1999: 10)

Reading 2.2

Observing and copying the day-to-day activities of parents helps children to make sense of the world they live in, and to feel part of that world by experiencing it at first hand. This helps children's creative imagination, which they can then apply in imaginary play; like an actor learning a part, the first step is to learn the words and actions, then rehearse, maybe improvise by adding an individual twist, and finally to perform.

(Dorman and Dorman 2002: 180)

Reading 2.3

The mother of a baby boy, Ralph, had no doubt but that Ralph loved his feeds. She had the impression of someone who concentrated intensely, who worked away at sucking who yet had enormous pleasure from many of his feeds. He would lie on her knee after the feed was over, mouthing and smiling. One day she saw something that took her attention. She went up to his pram. Ralph did not see her. He was looking intently up into the thick green leaves of a tree which overshadowed the pram. And he was making sucking movements with his mouth. It was as though he had something of the same experience from looking up at the green sunlit tree as he did at the breast. On another occasion she saw him do the same – attending and sucking – when his aunt played the piano. From many little examples like this we can see how responsive babies are to sensuous experiences that capture their attention and indeed move them deeply. The appreciation of beauty exists in babyhood.

(Miller 1992: 58–9)

Implications for practice

Questioning what we do

This sequence may prompt reflection on the choices that are made (sometimes without discussion or without input from the individuals most concerned) about the following:

1 *Is the outdoor environment* a rich resource or something we take for granted?

2 Do we believe in the value of *mixed-age groups* or do we think they're alright for others but would never work in our setting?

3 How would we respond to this argument about children's agendas:
'We believe in it, but we have to stick to our planning at all costs?'

3 Girl with book
Section A

At a drop-in facility within an Early Years Centre for parents and their children, staffed by several practitioners, Louise and her seventeen-month-old daughter, Grace, have been coming along to sessions for 10 months. They came originally for support with breast-feeding but now Louise has begun to bring Grace along to other sessions to help develop Grace's play, learning and social interaction.

Links

- DVD Chapter 3.
- Birth to Three Matters: A Skilful Communicator: Listening and Responding; A Competent Learner: Making Connections.
- Early Years Foundation Stage: Communication, Language and Literacy.

Discussion

After watching Chapter 3 of the DVD consider what issues the sequence raises regarding the following:

- How babies learn.
- Early literacy.
- Adult as a resource.

Readings

Reading 3.1

- Learning is a shared process and children learn most effectively when, with the support of a knowledgeable and trusted adult, they are actively involved and interested.
- Children learn when they are given appropriate responsibility, allowed to make errors, decisions and choices, and respected as autonomous and competent learners.
- Children learn by doing rather than by being told.

(DfES 2002: 5)

Reading 3.2

Planning for young children should be flexible – should flow with the child and may often be written retrospectively to describe and reflect on how what was planned followed a particular 'avenue of exploration' since the purpose of planning for babies and young children is not the demonstration of a particular practitioner's skill at crystal ball gazing. Rather it is an endeavour to project into how any child might be expected to engage with materials, activities and experiences through the involvement of a skilful and sensitive adult. The importance of this approach cannot be overstated.

(Abbott and Langston 2005: 73)

Reading 3.3

As babies and young children enjoy the pleasure of stories, songs, rhymes and jingles they learn to anticipate endings and play with words and sounds. These extend and build on cooing, vocalizing and babbling to skills such as inserting missing words in a well-known rhyme. Word play rapidly follows as children introduce variations on a theme to explore strings of sounds or words that have novelty value, such as the word 'woollies', used by one grandmother to describe sweaters and cardigans, which revealed her grandchildren's delight in this new word and which prompted 'much laughter and falling about, accompanied by repetitions of 'Woolly, woolly, woolly' (David et al. 2003: 81) from them. The latter illustrates clearly how through *Making Meaning* children play to learn and their delight in the novel sounds becomes

part of the process by which they develop an interest in rhyme and begin to make meaning when they encounter print in the environment, another example of becoming a skilful communicator.

(Abbott and Langston 2006: 33)

Implications for practice

This sequence could be used to prompt discussion on planning for individuals, especially:

- Knowledge of the child
  - from parents
  - from observation.
- Children's choices.
- Time allocation.

The photographs below could also be used to prompt discussion on planning for individuals:

Next Steps

After having looked at the book and listened to and joined in with the story Grace selected this book, from among others, set out at her height where she could easily find it, and began to explore it independently.

This is an example of 'the books or stories' she 'enjoys looking at independently'

(Look, listen, note: *A Skilful Communicator: Birth to Three Matters* (DfES 2002)).

4 Young baby with mirror and toy

Section A

A drop-in session for parents and children. The parent, Wendy, regularly attends drop-in and a parent group. She is also a governor of the centre. Here she is on a visit with her youngest child, Zara, aged eight months. At first Zara is interested in looking at herself in a mirror before Wendy extends her experience by introducing a toy for her to look at.

Links

- DVD Chapter 4.
- Birth to Three Matters: A Strong Child: Me, Myself and I, Being Acknowledged and Affirmed, Developing Self-assurance.
- Early Years Foundation Stage: Personal, Social and Emotional Development.

Discussion

After watching Chapter 4 of the DVD consider what issues the sequence raises regarding the following:

- Self and other.
- Sensitive adults.
- Knowing and communicating.

Readings

Reading 4.1

In the first year of life there is an increase in the complexity of a baby's internal and external world. Over the past months, the baby has been learning about the people around them via their faces, emotional expressiveness and behaviour. Inwardly the baby's brain has been sifting, sorting and filing the diverse stimuli, gradually organizing them into patterns of expected consequences, linking feelings with behaviour, culminating in the emergent comprehension of 'I' and 'you' through early 'conversations' and in the ability to share interest in a common stimulus such as a toy.

(Robinson 2003: 129)

Reading 4.2

Play episodes become quickly established between a baby and their carers through gentle caresses, light tickles, exaggerated facial expressions of amusement, surprise and so on. Even whilst feeding, the play behaviours, which adult and child build together, are important in establishing the kinds of play relationships which will develop later. As the baby becomes more able to participate and take control, the way in which a sensitive adult allows for this will influence the baby's feelings of efficacy. The adult behaving 'contingently', i.e. being responsive to the baby's signals, plays an important part in helping the baby to realise that they are able to influence their own lives and the behaviour of those around them.

Mirrors reflect the self back to the observer. The provision of mirrors in different places helps babies explore what they look like.

(Abbott and Langston 2006: 30)

Reading 4.3

Making sense of the world: people, emotions and beliefs

Immediately after birth the gradual understanding of what it is to be human appears to dawn, in a piecemeal way. Even the newly born, and certainly a month-old baby, will respond to overtures of communication by imitating any facial expressions made to her. Mouths will open and tongues protrude in perfect synchrony to a human partner. Slightly later than the physical gestures of interaction, the seemingly bizarre sounds adults are pre-programmed to make in order to engage an infant's attention (namely 'coos', 'goos' and 'oohs') are responded to and imitated. The communication is deeply and mutually satisfying and is the fore-runner to full-blown conversation. This work seems to indicate that babies are aware at birth that they are members of the human race and that a grasp of the art of social intercourse is an essential part of that membership.

(Riley 2003: 5)

Implications for practice

The photographs shown here were taken in the course of a day, and show Zara being held up in the arms of a practitioner; having a cuddle with the same practitioner; with another baby and adult and with her mum at the herb frame. Think about what they convey about:

- The baby's day.
- High quality resources.
- Emotional availability.

5 Boy in hammock
Section A

A drop-in facility for parents and their children, staffed by a number of practitioners. Lorraine and Caden, seventeen months, have been attending sessions at the drop-in since Caden was a few weeks old. Here he is engaged in a number of experiences with his mum.

Links

- DVD Chapter 5.
- Birth to Three Matters: A Skilful Communicator: Being Together, Listening and Responding, Making Meaning; A Competent Learner: Being Imaginative, Being Creative.
- Early Years Foundation Stage: Personal, Social and Emotional Development, Communication, Language and Literacy, Problem Solving, Reasoning and Numeracy.

Discussion

After watching Chapter 5 of the DVD consider what issues the sequence raises regarding the following:

- Relationships, especially with a key person.
- Observing and responding.
- Importance of interaction, talk, play.

Readings

Reading 5.1

Affection and attachment

Babies and very young children need warm, committed care and continuity. They exist most happily in relation to a small number of other people, with whom they seek to create intimate and intense relationships – relationships of attachment.

Children are cared for predominantly by one or two key persons and warm attachment is fostered

In a day care context, it is much easier to meet young children's need for warm, committed care and continuity if they are cared for predominantly by one or two key persons, rather than by the full range of the staff team. A child in a day care setting has been left by the parent – her main attachment relationship – to be cared for by others. In this situation, it is immensely reassuring for the child to know that she has a special person who knows her and her family, cares about her and will reliably respond to her needs.

Having a key person, to whom she has a real attachment, can ease a child's inevitable pain on being separated from her parent and form a secure bridge into the different world of daycare.

(Edwards 2002: 18, 20)

Reading 5.2

Observing so closely perhaps will sometimes feel as if it is observing too closely, that we are seeing right inside the child. Is seeing too much as bad as not seeing enough? Maybe the answer to this depends on the reasons for our 'seeing'. Are we observing to be voyeuristic, or intrusive, or are we observing in order to understand and use this understanding to help match our planning and responses to babies and very young children more effectively?

Observation can be double-edged and how it is undertaken, or not, the way we manage our encounters with the youngest children, is precisely what has been described as the 'ethics of an encounter' (Dahlberg et al. 1999: 106). The way we respond in our encounters with children, for example how much time we give to observing, what we are prepared to see or what we

can tolerate to notice, all are part of our subjective responses. One way of thinking about the ethics of our encounters with children is to think about these subjective responses.

(Elfer 2005: 127)

Reading 5.3

Between approximately 9-months, and two-years-old infants develop a shared understanding and memory that allows a growing capacity for symbolic coding of ideas and classification into categories. Along with a growing vocabulary they build a repertoire of gestures, behaviours and imitations. Schemas or habitual ways of acting and understanding also develop. During their second year infants can display great pleasure when showing and talking about their discoveries and they enjoy imitating their peers. They are very sensitive to social manners and customs, making them more aware of differences among the members of social groups they experience. Research has also shown that at around 18-20 months children develop a new awareness of the meanings of others and can react emotionally to this, for example becoming fearful if misunderstood or confused by conflicting meanings in what people say or do. Similarly they can be disturbed by differences between the emotional relationships they experience at home and in out-of-home provision.

(Scottish Executive Education Department 2003: 2–3)

Implications for Practice

Given what this sequence shows about the way adults mediate young children's experiences, consider what it means to know a child well. What are the features of such a relationship?

How does knowing a child well translate into practice in your setting? How are individual needs catered for?

6 Boy with book

Section A

A drop-in facility for parents and their children, staffed by a number of practitioners. Lorraine and Caden, seventeen months, have been attending sessions in drop-in since Caden was a few weeks old. Here he is sharing a book with his mum.

Links

- DVD Chapter 6.
- Birth to Three Matters: A Strong Child: Developing Self-assurance; A Skilful Communicator: Being Together, Listening and Responding.
- Early Years Foundation Stage: Personal, Social and Emotional Development, Communication, Language and Literacy.

Discussion

After watching Chapter 6 of the DVD consider what issues the sequences raises about:

- The importance of interaction, talk, play.
- Joint engagement.
- Meaningful literacy experiences for young children.

Readings

Reading 6.1

Talking and reading with toddlers is the best way to help them extend their language. You can talk with children about many things. They are very interested in themselves and their activities! Adults and older children can describe for them in words what they are doing, hearing, seeing, touching, tasting, smelling and feeling.

There seems to be an explosion of vocabulary between about 18 and 22 months. This may be because children become aware that everything has a name. This is the time when the constantly repeated cry of 'What's that?' can drive adults to distraction. However, patience is rewarded as communication increases, along with the child's language. Children's increased memory ability helps them with long words, even if they don't always come out correctly. Ben's version of 'hippopotamus' came out as 'pitohapamus'. He had the right number of syllables and all the right sounds, but not the order. Children have enough grammar now to get their meaning across to an adult who knows them well and listens attentively.

(Makin and Whitehead 2004: 32)

Reading 6.2

While literacy and play were conceived of as totally different objects, there were emerging some similarities. It was now possible to view both play and literate behaviours as under the control of children. It was possible to see in both that children engaged with a rich variety of world experiences and knowledge, rather than limiting themselves to those things conventionally seen as appropriate to children. To be young was not to be without means of engaging with the world in all its complexities.

(Hall and Robinson 1988: 8)

Reading 6.3

Mrs Tulley says, returning to the bench, 'It's a mystery, don't you think? I mean the way these babies take to story telling it's like they were born doing it.' Funny thing, most folks I meet at conferences don't even know the twos can do it. Even though it's nothing different than play.

(Gussin-Paley 2001: 7)

Implications for practice

This sequence could be used to consider the role of language and communication in literacy development.

You may also wish to think about the following:

Adults' knowledge of meaningful literacy practices with babies and toddlers

- What is effective literacy practice for babies and toddlers?
- Where could you find out more about the relationship between speaking, listening, reading and writing?

High quality resources

- What value do we place on providing high quality resources for babies and young children? Why?
- How can we build, on or give more attention to our resources to ensure they are of high quality all the time?

Babies and books

- How are we involved in programmes and/ or with other professionals in providing for babies' and young children's communication, language and literacy development?
  - What is the distinct contribution we make to babies' and young children's communication, language and literacy development?

7 Toddlers playing
Section A

Grace who is seventeen months old has struck up a friendship with Caden, a seventeen-month-old boy. Their mums are friendly because they have attended drop-in at the Early Years Centre together since their babies were very young. When they play together one of their mums keeps watch and joins in when invited, while the other one sits nearby.

Links

- DVD Chapter 7.
- Birth to Three Matters: A Strong Child: Developing Self-assurance, A Sense of Belonging; A Competent Learner: Being Creative; A Healthy Child: Emotional Well-being; Growing and Developing.
- Early Years Foundation Stage: Personal, Social and Emotional Development, Knowledge and Understanding of the World.

Discussion

After watching Chapter 7 of the DVD consider what issues the sequence raises regarding the following:

- Child relationships.
- Engaging with children's emotions and play.
- Being imaginative.

Readings

Reading 7.1

Engaging with babies is crucial not only for obtaining a fuller empirical picture of infant development, but also for the infant's development itself – for well being, learning and teaching (Bruner 1996; Hobson 2002; Rogoff, Paradise, Arauz, Correa-Chavez, & Angelillo, 2003; Trevarthen, 2001, in press). Our responses within engagement enable us to notice and interpret infants' specific behaviours and to recognize and legitimize these behaviours. When we engage and respond to someone, we are entering a shared reality in which each person can share in the other's behaviour. Consider this example:

A 12-month-old infant is sitting on his mother's lap, looking out of the window, and he sees a flock of birds fly up in a rush. He points to them excitedly, vocally exclaiming and with both arms extended, but not turning around to look at his mother. His mother looks too, and says, in a lively, confirming way, 'Oh yes! Isn't that exciting?' The infant leans back into his mother's body and continues to watch the birds.

Her reaction – from the tone in her voice and the movement of her body – affirms her son's excitement and legitimises his act of communication about the birds. Her response celebrates their companionship as they gain knowledge about the world and experience the emotions that such learning can stir (Dissanayke, 2000; Hobson, 2002). The simple example of a mother and her son discovering a flock of birds suggests that if an infant does not receive an emotional reaction to his emotions, he might stop expressing them or he might not experience them in quite the same way.

(Reddy and Trevarthen 2004: 9–17)

Reading 7.2

Bowlby (1969) describes how maintaining the equilibrium of the relationship between adult and child, through being caring, sensitive, available and responsive, allows the child to develop an attachment relationship with the adult. Children who have secure attachment relationships are more able to be independent, to relate to their peers and engage in more complex and creative play. Such children are more flexible and resourceful and have higher self-esteem.

(Schaffer and Emerson 1964: Section 1, Page 2)

Reading 7.3

By encouraging creativity and imagination we are promoting children's ability to explore and comprehend their world and increasing their opportunities to make new connections and reach new understandings. Young children are naturally curious about the people and the world around them and they want to know more about their relationship to them. Through their imagination children can move from the present into the past and the future to what might be and beyond. They are freed from the world of immediate sensations.

(Duffy 1998: 8)

Implications for Practice

Use the Observation Sheet (Figure 7.1) to review Chapter 7 of the DVD, noting what features of the engagement between adult and child seem to support the child in their explorations, interactions and investigations.

Consider how the nature of adult interaction in your setting influences children's exploration and investigation.

Child's Name:	Name of adult with child:	Date:
Context:		
What does the child do?	**What does the adult do to support the child?**	**How do the responses of the adult and the child affect the behaviour of one another?**

Figure 7.1 Observation sheet

8 Emily and her mum
Section A

A drop-in facility within an Early Years Centre for parents and their children, staffed by several practitioners. Emily and her mum, Helen, visit occasionally when Helen is not working.

Links

- DVD Chapter 8.
- Birth to Three Matters: A Strong Child: Being Acknowledged and Affirmed, Developing Self-assurance; A Skilful Communicator: Being Together; A Competent Learner: Being Creative; A Healthy Child: Emotional Well-being, Growing and Developing, Keeping Safe.
- Early Years Foundation Stage: Personal, Social and Emotional Development, Problem Solving, Reasoning and Numeracy, Knowledge and Understanding of the World.

Discussion

After watching Chapter 8 of the DVD consider what issues the sequence raises regarding the following:

- Appropriate activities, experiences.
- Feelings and emotions.
- Supportive relationships.

Readings

Reading 8.1

Babies need genuine acceptance – mothers and other important people cannot pretend. There is a very early balancing act in the interaction between the mother and baby: as the mother consciously and unconsciously shows the baby what she recognises and accepts, the baby learns to *be* the sort of person she will recognise and accept. If she is able to recognise and accept *all* the baby's feelings as important, then the baby will be able to recognise and accept them also. The baby's developing self-perception reflects that he or she is growing into a whole person who has a mixture of feelings. Initially, a mother may accept, and thus hold, some feelings for the baby until they are manageable. Then there will come a time when, because the baby *can* accept feelings of pain, anxiety and anger as genuine and legitimate, he or she can begin to learn to deal with them.

We often talk, though, of babies as being good, lovable, awful, or difficult. All the time, and unavoidably, we give babies and young children signals about what we love in them, what we approve of and how we want them to be. It is a natural way of showing them how to be acceptable, both to us and to the world in general. The child's developing self-perception is inextricably linked with learning to be acceptable; but being acceptable sometimes means not showing pain, fear or anger. So it happens that some children learn to exclude pain, fear and anger from their perceptions of themselves: unable either to control those feelings or have them safely accepted by someone else, they manage to 'lose' them in order to be acceptable.

(Roberts 2002: 9)

Reading 8.2

'I' and 'you' is also 'we'. Up to this point, the baby can only understand others via their external behaviours – now comes the first glimmerings of understanding that others have an internal world too. The baby has also learned to look to familiar carers to give clues to the acceptability or otherwise of new experiences and new people … Clues to how to react come from social referencing where the infant looks to the adult for guidance and reassurance.

(Robinson 2003: 129–130)

Reading 8.3

Each infant or toddler has a unique way of acting or interacting and does so on his or her own timetable. An older infant, Michelle, for example, initiates a game of scarf peek-a-boo with her caregiver. Natalie, an infant of about the same age, watches the game with interest but does not join in, even when the caregiver offers her a scarf. Her caregiver, however, accepts Natalie's response, realising, that Natalie *has*, in a sense, joined the game simply by choosing to watch it.

Caregivers also understand that infants and toddlers, craving repetition, often spend a long time repeating an enjoyable action – banging a spoon, turning the pages of a board book, filling and emptying a basket of shells. Therefore, caregivers might play endless games of peek-a-boo with children or willingly look at their favourite books or read their favourite stories again and again, because they understand that with child-initiated repetition comes understanding and mastery.

(Post and Hohmann 2000: 69–70)

Implications for practice

Consider ways in which the following photographs exemplify the statements in either Reading 8.1 or 8.2.

What are the implications of your findings for practice?

References

Abbott, L. and Langston, A. (eds) (2005) *Birth to Three Matters: Supporting the Framework of Effective Practice*. Maidenhead: Open University Press.

Abbott, L. and Langston, A. (2006) Learning to play, playing to learn, in J. Moyles (ed.) *The Excellence of Play*, 2nd edn. Maidenhead: Open University Press.

Adamson, L.B., Bakeman, R. and Deckner, D.F. (2004) The development of symbol-infused joint engagement, *Child Development*, 75(4): 1171–87.

Athey, C. (1990) *Extending Thought in Young Children: A Parent–Teacher Partnership*. London: Paul Chapman.

Dorman, H. and Dorman, C. (2002) *The Social Toddler: Promoting Positive Behaviour*. London: The Children's Project.

Duffy, B. (1998) *Supporting Creativity and Imagination in the Early Years*. Buckingham: Open University Press.

DfES (2002) *Birth to Three Matters*. London: DfES.

DfES (2006) *Early Years Foundation Stage* (Consultation document). London: DfES.

Edwards, A.G. (2002) *Relationships and Learning: Caring for Children from Birth to Three*. London: National Children's Bureau.

Elfer, P. (2005) Observation matters, in L. Abbott and A. Langston. (eds) *Birth to Three Matters: Supporting the Framework of Effective Practice*. Maidenhead: Open University Press.

Gussin-Paley, V. (2001) *In Mrs Tulley's Room: A Childcare Portrait*. Harvard, CT: Harvard University Press.

Hall, N. and Robinson, A. (1988) *Exploring Writing and Play in the Early Years*. London: David Fulton.

HM Treasury (2004) *Choice for Parents, the Best Start for Children: A Ten Year Strategy for Childcare*. Norwich: The Stationery Office.

International Attachment Network (2002) www.attachmentnetwork.org/links.html

Langston, A. (2003) Get settled, Nursery Business, *Nursery World* (Autumn).

Laevers, F. (1997/2004) The innovative project: experiential education and the definition of quality in education in R. Forbes (ed.) *Beginning to Play: Young Children from Birth to Three*. Maidenhead: Open University Press.

Makin, L. and Whitehead, M. (2004) *Children's Early Literacy: A Guide for Professional Carers and Educators*. London: Paul Chapman.

Manning-Morton, J. and Thorp, M. (2003) *Key Times for Play: The First Three Years*. Maidenhead: Open University Press.

Miller, L. (1992) *Understanding Your Baby*. London: The Rosendale Press.

Nutbrown, C. (1999) *Threads of Thinking,* 2nd edn. London: Paul Chapman.

Post, J. and Hohmann, M. (2000) *Tender Care and Early Learning*. Michigan: High Scope Press.

Reddy, V. and Trevarthen, C. (2004) What we learn about babies from engaging with their emotions, *Zero to Three*, 24(3): 9–17.

Riley, J. (2003) *Learning in the Early Years*. London: Paul Chapman.

Roberts, R. (2002) *Self-esteem and Early Learning,* 2nd edn. London: Paul Chapman.

Robinson, M. (2003) *From Birth to One: The Year of Opportunity*. Buckingham: Open University Press.

Schaffer, H.R. and Emerson, P.F. (1964) The development of social attachments in infancy, *Monographs of the Research in Child Development*, 29 (Serial No. 94).

Scottish Executive Education Department (2003) *Insight 6: Meeting the Needs of Children Birth to Three: Research Evidence and Implications for Out-of-home Provision*. Edinburgh: Scottish Executive Education Department. http://www.scotland.gov.uk/Publications/2003/06/17458/22696

Sylva, K., Melhuish, E., Sammons, P., Siraj-Blatchford, I. and Taggart, B. (2004) *The Effective Provision of Pre-school Education (EPPE) Project Final Report*. London: DfES.